THE BEST ONLINE

JOBS FOR TEENS

Your sure way to earn money

online from home

Written By

Ihekwoaba Joseph

TABLE OF CONTENTS

CHAPTER 1

Introduction to Online Jobs for Teenagers

The best online jobs for teens

The term "online jobs" describes work completed remotely over the internet. These positions frequently allow workers to determine their schedules and the freedom to work from any location with an internet connection. They are a choice that individuals of all ages, especially teenagers, are choosing more frequently.

You might be a teen seeking methods to make extra money at home. You may find that working online is a terrific alternative because you can set your schedule and pace.

We will examine some of the top teen-friendly internet occupations in this book so you can make money from the convenience of your home.

Online jobs help meet your requirements and interests, whether you're aiming to earn a little extra money on the side or you need a full-time income.

Many online occupations can provide you the chance to make money while still in school or in your leisure time, ranging from freelance writing and social media management to customer service and data entry.

The specifics of these online occupations, such as the knowledge and experience needed, the kinds of work performed, and the possible pay for each position, will be covered in more detail in this guide.

Additionally, we will offer advice and tools to get you started on your search for the ideal online position.

Advantages of online jobs for teens

Online employment for teens has many benefits, including:

1. Flexibility: Working online helps you to have the freedom to set your hours, which is very helpful for teenagers juggling extracurricular activities and school.

2. Convenience: With an online job, you may work from home or on the go as long as you have an internet connection.

3. Developing your skills: Online jobs require skills such as writing, graphic design, or customer service, which can give you significant experience and make you stand out in the job market.

4. Earning potential: Depending on the position, you might be able to make a respectable living from working online.

5. No commute: Working online eliminates the need for public transportation, which can save time and money.

6. Greater accessibility: For people who live in remote regions or have disabilities that make it challenging to work outside the home, online employment is frequently more accessible.

Disadvantages of online jobs for teens

Online employment for teenagers may have some drawbacks, including the following:

1. Limited chances: Teens may have fewer online work prospects than adults if the position necessitates knowledge or abilities that teens may not yet possess.

2. Age limitations: It could be difficult for teenagers to find acceptable employment due to age restrictions on some internet jobs.

3. Lack of monitoring: It may be difficult for teenagers to stay on target and fulfill deadlines when they work online because there is likely less oversight than there would be at regular employment.

4. Limited social engagement: Some kids may feel isolated by the lack of social interaction and teamwork associated with online jobs compared to traditional occupations.

5. Possibility of scams: Teens should exercise caution and due diligence before accepting any job offers because there is a chance that they will come across scammers while hunting for internet employment.

6. Limited benefits: Internet employment does not provide perks like healthcare or retirement plans.

Why online jobs are a vital option for teens

There are several reasons why teens should consider working online:

1. Work experience: Online employment can help teenagers gain essential work experience and hone crucial abilities like time management, communication, and problem-solving.

2. Additional income: Teens who work online may earn additional revenue that they can use to save money, pay for education, or cover other costs.

3. Possibility to pick up new skills: Many online jobs call for technology and may entail acquiring new ones for professional and personal growth.

4. Variety of employment opportunities: Teens can discover an online job that suits their interests and abilities

thanks to the wide range of available employment opportunities.

The benefits of working from home

The following are some advantages of working from home:

1. Flexibility: Working from home gives you more control over your schedule and can help you more easily juggle work and other obligations.

2. Financial savings: By working from home, you can avoid paying for transportation, gas, and other expenses linked to commuting to an office.

3. Enhanced productivity: Due to fewer interruptions and distractions, several people feel that working from home increases their productivity.

4. Comfort: Working from home allows you to do it in a familiar and comfortable setting, which might be enticing if you have a home office or other designated workspace.

5. Better work-life balance: Since working from home allows you to manage your time and schedule, it can help you strike a better balance between your professional and personal lives.

CHAPTER 2

Online Freelancing Jobs for Teens

Freelancing jobs

When someone works as a freelancer, they do so on a project-by-project basis rather than being a full-time employee of an organization. Freelancers are often compensated by project or an hour and are in charge of finding their clients and managing their schedules.

Types of Skills in Demand for Freelancers

For freelancers, the following talents are in high demand:

• Writing and editing: Writers and editors are always in demand since business owners require quality content for their websites, marketing materials, and other uses.

• Graphic design: Designers of visual material are required to produce infographics, social media graphics, and logos.

• Technical expertise: Freelancers with technical expertise can find work in many industries.

• Customer service: Some businesses use independent contractors to serve as customer service representatives, fielding inquiries and grievances from clients via phone, email, or chat.

How to Start a Freelance Career

It can be scary to start as a freelancer, but everyone has to start somewhere. You can start by following these steps:

• Identify your experience and skills: Think about your strengths and passions. It will enable you to choose the freelancing positions that might be a good fit for you.

• Create a portfolio of your work. Showcase your abilities to potential clients by using a portfolio of your work.

• Establish a freelance business: To handle your finances and safeguard your legal rights, think about establishing a formal business structure, such as a sole proprietorship or Limited Liability Company (LLC).

• Marketing: Getting new clients for your services requires effective marketing. You can locate clients by using social media, networking, or job boards.

Tips for Succeeding as a Freelancer

Here are some pointers to help you be a successful freelancer:

• Establish clear boundaries: It's crucial to establish clear boundaries with your clients as a freelancer to make time for other obligations and prevent burnout.

• Provide high-quality work: Your reputation as a freelancer is your most precious asset, so it's critical to provide high-quality work on time to earn your client's trust.

• Communicate effectively: Effective communication is essential for freelance success, keep your clients updated on your work and respond to any queries or issues they may have.

• Be proactive: Reach out to potential clients and introduce yourself; don't wait for business to come to you.

Where to Look for Freelance Work

Finding freelance work can be done in many ways, such as

• Freelance job websites: Numerous freelance job possibilities are available on websites like Upwork and Fiverr and other industries.

• Professional networking can help you get freelance work because other professionals in your sector may be able to recommend you for jobs or put you in touch with possible clients.

• Personal website: Showcasing your abilities on a personal website or online portfolio will assist you with clients.

• Social media: Sites like LinkedIn and Twitter are popular places for freelancers to look for work.

Website for teens who freelance

Teens can find freelancing opportunities on a variety of websites. A few choices are as follows:

1. Upwork is a well-known website for freelancers of all ages. With categories like writing, design, and customer service, you can find a range of projects.

2. Fiverr: This website enables you to market your freelancing skills, including writing, graphic design, and video editing.

3. Freelancer: This website offers a variety of tasks, such as social media management, website creation, and data input.

4. PeoplePerHour: This website features a selection of freelancing positions, such as marketing, writing, and translation work.

5. 99designs: If you possess creative talent, this platform enables you to participate in design competitions and earn money for your efforts.

Remember to check the terms of service before creating an account on any of these platforms, as some may have age limitations.

CHAPTER 3

Online Survey and Market Research Jobs for Teens

A technique for getting data from people online is through surveys. Surveys can be via several different channels, such as email, social media, and websites.

They include questions on various subjects, including political opinions, media consumption patterns, and consumer preferences.

Businesses, organizations, and researchers frequently use surveys to obtain information and understanding about a group or market.

The process of gathering and analyzing data regarding a particular market or business is known as market research. Market research is to inform business and marketing strategies. It may incorporate a variety of approaches, such as focus groups, interviews, and case studies.

Market research can be used to uncover opportunities and obstacles in a given market and helps firms better understand the needs, behaviors, and preferences of their target audience.

How to get started with online surveys and market research

1. Look for businesses online that conduct market research studies and paid surveys.

2. Open a profile with an organization reputable in surveys or market research.

3. Fill out the profile. You have a better chance of being chosen for research if your profile meets the requirements.

4. Keep an eye out for announcements regarding open studies in your inbox and on the corporate website.

5. Finish the assigned studies following the given guidance. Throughout your comments, be truthful and comprehensive.

6. After reaching the minimum payment threshold, cash out your earnings. Depending on the business, this threshold could be different.

It's crucial to keep in mind that each organization may have different minimum age restrictions and pay scales. Some businesses might have prerequisites or qualifications for surveys or market research studies.

To improve your chances of being chosen for studies, ensure to adhere to the directions offered by each firm.

Examples of survey and market research companies that hire teens

Companies that engage teenagers for surveys and market research include the following:

• Swagbucks: Swagbucks is a business that compensates customers for online shopping, watching videos, and other activities. Teens 13 years of age and older can open a Swagbucks account and begin earning rewards.

• Survey Junkie: This company compensates consumers for their comments in surveys. Teens 13 years old and older can sign up for Survey Junkie and begin taking surveys.

• Harris Poll Online: Harris Poll Online is a market research firm that holds focus groups and surveys on various subjects. Participants in Harris Poll Online research must be at least 14 years old.

• American Consumer Opinion is a market research organization that pays customers for feedback on goods and services. Teens 13 and older can sign up for American Consumer Opinion and begin taking surveys and participating in focus groups.

CHAPTER 4

Social Media Management Jobs for Teens

The process of developing, planning, analyzing, and interacting with information shared on social media channels is known as social media management. It entails creating and putting social media marketing plans and keeping track of and reacting to user involvement.

Modern business requires social media management since it enables communication with customers, brand promotion, and increased online visibility.

The function of social media in modern business

Social media today serves the purpose of helping businesses connect with and interact with their target audience. It is possible by producing and disseminating worthwhile and pertinent material and answering their questions and messages.

Social media is a crucial tool for customer service as it enables businesses to reply to questions and concerns from customers quickly.

Businesses utilize social media not just to engage with customers but also to advertise their goods and services, as well as to develop their brand and reputation. In addition to gathering customer insights and feedback, social media management is to assess how well marketing efforts are working.

Social media today primarily serves the purposes of connecting with customers, promoting a business and its goods, and gathering insightful data.

List of teen careers in social media management

Teenagers can work in various social media management positions, including part-time jobs, freelancing, and internships. Teenagers may be in charge of doing the following duties when managing social media:

1. Writing and planning posts on social media sites, including Facebook, Instagram, and Twitter.

2. Examining social media indicators like likes, comments, and shares to gauge the success of campaigns and content

3. Engaging with users through likes and comments, responding to comments and messages.

4. Creating social media marketing tactics, such as target audience identification, content calendar creation, and ideal posting times.

5. Working with other team members to develop and carry out social media initiatives such as graphic designers and content producers.

6. Remaining current on the newest social media trends and best practices.

Social media intern, social media assistant, or social media coordinator are a few possible career titles for teenagers interested in social media administration.

The expertise required to handle social media

1. Excellent written and verbal communication abilities: Since managing social media sometimes requires writing, it is crucial to have these skills.

2. Creativity: For social media material to be fascinating and engaging, it is crucial to have the capacity for original thought.

3. Knowledge of social media platforms: It's crucial to grasp the various platform of social media, their capabilities, and how to use them successfully for marketing.

4. Basic graphic design abilities: Creating aesthetically appealing material is essential for capturing readers' attention. It is vital to be familiar with design programs like Adobe Creative Suite.

5. Analytical abilities: Social media management requires data and metrics to gauge the performance of campaigns and glean information about user behavior.

6. Organizational abilities: Managing social media frequently entails juggling several projects and due dates, so it's critical to be well-organized and able to set priorities.

7. Marketing knowledge: Being familiar with marketing fundamentals and how to use them in a social media setting is helpful.

What it takes to become a social media manager

Consider performing the following actions to begin working as a social media manager:

1. Acquire experience: Consider acquiring skills through internships or by offering your services to handle the social media accounts of a club or group at your school.

Along with giving you significant experience, this will also help to create your portfolio and demonstrate your talents and abilities to potential employers.

2. Establish a powerful online presence by setting up a professional social media profile and providing pertinent and engaging information.

It helps you position yourself as a thought leader in your industry and show prospective employers your level of skills.

3. Study social media marketing: Spend time studying the fundamentals and best practices of social media marketing. It is possible by taking online classes, seminars, workshops, or reading articles and blog postings on the sector.

4. Put together a portfolio of your work to show prospective employers your abilities and experience. Examples of social media campaigns you have worked on, statistics showing the effectiveness of your efforts, and any other pertinent work are all examples.

5. Search for job openings: To uncover social media management job openings, think about contacting nearby companies or browsing online job ads. To improve your chances of landing a job, it's also a good idea to network with professionals in the field and go to job fairs.

In conclusion, launching a career as a social media manager necessitates a mix of obtaining knowledge, establishing a solid online presence, studying social media marketing, developing a portfolio, and actively looking for employment openings.

Tips for finding and succeeding in social media management work

The following are some pointers for locating and excelling at social media management jobs:

1. Develop your skills: Learn social media platforms, marketing concepts, and best practices. To increase knowledge, enroll in online classes, workshops, and seminars.

2. Network with industry experts: Go to industry events and conferences, get in touch with experts on social media management and improve your chances of getting hired.

3. Be proactive in your job search. Look for openings by contacting nearby companies or browsing internet job boards. Applying for internships or entry-level jobs is a great choice to develop your resume and experience.

4. Keep up with the most recent trends and best practices: It's critical to keep up with the most recent trends and best practices if you want to be successful with social media management.

It helps to maintain an active social media presence, consistently producing and disseminating material and responding quickly to user feedback and communications.

5. Establish clear goals and constantly assess your progress: It's crucial to establish precise goals and your progress when developing and maintaining social media campaigns.

Guidelines for establishing and running social media campaigns

Following are some guidelines for developing and running social media campaigns:

1. Establish specific objectives: It is vital to define your desired outcomes. Do you want to engage your audience, boost sales, or raise brand awareness?

Having a goal can assist direct your campaign plan and allow you to assess its effectiveness.

2. Specify your target audience: Think about the people for the campaign. What requirements and interests do they have? What platforms do they use for social media? It helps to generate material that appeals to your target audience by understanding who they are.

3. Create a content calendar: Arrange the posts you'll make during your campaign, including the messages you want to get across and the kinds of content to publish. You can stay organized and make sure you're posting entertaining and pertinent material regularly by using a content calendar.

4. Use hashtags to help users find your brand and to boost your content.

5. Examine your findings: Track the success of your campaign and learn more about user behavior using tools like analytics. You can use this to determine what is effective and what could use improvement.

6. Interact with your audience: Promote user interaction by replying to comments from users and liking and commenting on their postings. It promotes brand community building and may boost client loyalty.

Setting clear objectives, identifying your target audience, planning a content calendar, utilizing hashtags, analyzing outcomes, communicating with your audience, and staying current with trends is necessary when creating and maintaining social media campaigns.

CHAPTER 5

Online Tutoring and Teaching Jobs for Teens

Giving pupils academic support and instruction online is known as online tutoring and teaching. It could involve private lessons, leading a class, or running an online school.

In addition to enabling students to obtain assistance and instruction from the convenience of their own homes, online tutoring and teaching help instructors to reach a larger audience and potentially work with students from various regions. Both students and teachers can study and teach using this flexible and practical method.

Examples of online tutoring and teaching jobs for teens

Teens can find a wide range of online tutoring and teaching positions. Here are a few instances:

1. One-on-one tutoring: In this profession, an adolescent assists one student in understanding a subject or boosting their grades. Video calls, chats, or screen sharing aid the learning process.

2. Group tutoring: A youngster who works in this line of activity collaborates with a small group of students to impart knowledge and offer support. It can be through online courses or video conferencing.

3. Online teaching: In this field, a teen designs and imparts knowledge via an online course on a topic. It can be via an online course platform or a website that focuses on providing online courses.

4. Test preparation tutoring: Many teenagers have subject-specific expertise and may provide test preparation tutoring to assist kids in getting ready for exams like the ACT, SAT, or GRE.

5. Homework assistance: Some teenagers may assist pupils who require it.

6. Language tutoring: Teens who are proficient in a second language can help pupils who are learning the language by tutoring them in that language.

7. Tutoring for kids with special needs: Adolescents with experience dealing with students who have disabilities may provide customized tutoring services for students who have learning difficulties or other special needs.

Skills needed for online tutoring

1. Time management: Online tutoring calls for the capacity to successfully manage your time and adhere to deadlines.

2. Ability to adapt to various learning styles and change your teaching strategies as necessary might be helpful while providing online tutoring.

3. Computer proficiency: You'll probably use video conferencing software and other online resources if you're an online tutor, so you should be comfortable utilizing computer programs and technology.

4. Patience: Online tutoring can be challenging at times, and it's crucial to have the patience to work with pupils and aid in their understanding of complex ideas.

5. Organizational capabilities: To be successful as an online tutor, you must stay on your schedule and remember vital appointments.

6. Communication abilities: You will be working with students remotely and may not have the chance to meet in person. The ability to communicate is crucial for online tutoring.

7. Creativity: In online tutoring, innovative and fresh ways to engage and inspire students is vital.

8. Empathy: Fostering a good and encouraging learning environment can be accomplished by demonstrating empathy and understanding for your pupils and their various learning requirements.

Types of subjects to teach as a teenage online tutor

You might be able to teach a variety of courses which include:

1. Math: Tutoring in math is frequently in great demand. Math is at various levels, from basic computation to advanced calculus.

2. Science: There are different levels of science courses, including biology, chemistry, and physics.

3. Language: If you speak a second language well, you might be able to help students study it by providing tutoring in that language.

4. Test preparation: To get ready for exams like the ACT, SAT, or GRE, many students hire test preparation teachers.

5. English: To assist pupils in developing their reading, writing, and grammar abilities, you can provide English tutoring services.

6. History: If you have a great understanding of history, you may be able to offer instruction on this topic.

7. Music: If you are talented in the musical arts, you might be able to provide teaching in guitar, piano, or singing.

8. Art: If you have artistic talent, you could be able to provide art education in disciplines like sculpture, painting, or sketching.

It is crucial to pick a subject you are knowledgeable about and passionate about because this will make it simpler to inspire your students.

How to get started as an online tutor

There are a few actions you can do to begin working as an online tutor:

1. The area of discipline is defined. It will enable you to choose the correct kind of tutoring or teaching position for you.

2. Increase your knowledge and proficiency in the subjects you are interested in tutoring or teaching. It can entail enrolling in classes or obtaining credentials.

3. Make a portfolio for your teaching or tutoring. It consists of your resume, a summary of your education and experience, and your abilities and certifications.

4. Begin promoting your services in your community or on tutoring websites. To advertise your abilities and services, you might do this by developing a website or social media pages.

5. Follow up with potential customers and be ready to haggle your prices and availability.

Online tutoring website

Teens can get careers as online teachers and tutors on several websites, including:

1. Tutor.com: Tutor.com is a platform for online tutoring that links students and tutors in various subject areas. There is no set minimum age limit for pupils, but tutors must be at least 18 years old.

2. Chegg: Chegg is a platform for online tuition that provides one-on-one tutoring in various areas. There is no set minimum age limit for pupils, but tutors must be at least 18 years old.

3. Wyzant: Wyzant is an online tutoring platform with the freedom for tutors to choose their fees and availability.

There is no set minimum age limit for pupils, but tutors must be at least 18 years old.

4. TutorMe: This online tutoring service provides instruction in various areas, including math, science, and language. Students have no set age restrictions, but tutors must be at least 18 years old.

5. Varsity Tutors: This online tutoring service provides tutoring in various areas, including math, science, and language. Students have no set age restrictions, but tutors must be at least 18 years old.

To find a tutoring platform, it is vital to research available options. Before registering, read the small print and comprehend the terms and conditions because some websites could have unique requirements or restrictions for tutors.

CHAPTER 6

Online Data Entry and Transcription Jobs for Teens

Online data entry involves entering information into a computer or other electronic device remotely, usually through the internet. Transcribing audio or video content into a textual form, entering data into a spreadsheet, or typing text into a word processor are all examples of data entry.

Converting audio or video content into written form is known as transcription. It includes watching a video while typing out the spoken words or listening to an audio tape and typing the spoken words.

Examples of online data entry and transcription jobs for teens

Teens can find various online data entry and transcription jobs, while the qualifications for each position may differ depending on the organization.

Teenagers may find it appropriate to work at online data entry and transcription jobs like these:

• Data entry clerks are responsible for entering data into computers or other electronic systems. It entails typing text, numbers, or symbols into a word processor, spreadsheet, or other software.

• Transcriptionist: A transcriptionist convert audio or video content into written text. It involves watching a video and typing the spoken words or listening to an audio recording and doing the same.

• A captioner: A captioner is in charge of producing closed captions for videos. It entails utilizing specialized software to watch a video while typing the spoken words in real-time.

• Social media manager: This person is in charge of looking after a company's social media accounts. It entails updating accounts, answering messages and comments, and keeping an eye on account activity.

• Customer service representative: A customer service person is responsible for assisting customers with their inquiries or issues over the phone, via email, or through online chat.

• Virtual assistant: A virtual assistant help a business owner or individual with various activities, including making travel arrangements, organizing appointments, and responding to emails.

Start by examining job boards or freelance marketplaces like Upwork or Freelancer to find teen-friendly data entry and transcription jobs online. It is vital to inquire about these positions with nearby firms or organizations.

Tips for finding and succeeding in online data entry and transcription work

There are a few things you can do to find online data entry and transcribing work:

1. Look for data entry and transcription positions on job search engines like Indeed, Monster, and LinkedIn.

Additionally, you might look at services like Upwork and Fiverr.

2. Create a resume and cover letter of data entry or transcribing position of your choice. If you have any relevant experience or talents, emphasize them.

3. As well as any required software or equipment, be sure you have a dependable computer and internet connection.

4. Be precise in your work and pay attention to the little things. High levels of precision are vital for data entry and transcription work.

5. Stick to deadlines and produce top-notch work. Keep a positive reputation and obtain repeat business or favorable testimonials.

6. Maintain organization and use time management skills. Working on numerous tasks is common in data entry and transcription professions, so the ability to set priorities and manage your workload is essential.

CHAPTER 7

Online Customer Service and Support Jobs for Teens

Online customer service and support refer to helping a business offer to its customers online. It includes using social media, email, live chat, or other types of communication, as well as having access to a website's knowledge base or frequently asked questions (FAQ) section.

In addition to enhancing the overall customer experience, online customer service and support promptly and effectively address any issues or concerns that customers may have.

Examples of online customer service and support jobs for teens

Listed below are a few examples of online customer care and support positions:

1. Live chat support: Live chat assist business and provide a fantastic entry point for youngsters into the customer service industry. You will be in charge of addressing client queries and issues via live chat in this position.

2. Support for social media: Many companies are active on sites like Facebook, Twitter, and Instagram. It involves reacting to consumer questions and grievances on various channels as a social media support professional.

3. Email support: Many companies get a lot of emails from customers with questions or concerns. It is vital to respond to client queries immediately.

4. Knowledge base writer: Some businesses employ adolescents to create and maintain FAQ or knowledge base sections on their websites. You would be in charge of conducting research for and creating articles that assist clients in finding the answers to their inquiries.

It's crucial to keep in mind that many of these occupations can require you to work remotely and that you might need a dependable internet connection and computer to complete them.

The responsibilities of an online customer service representative

Depending on the firm and function, the duties of an online customer care representative may vary, but some typical tasks and responsibilities may include

1. Quickly and professionally responding to consumer questions and grievances via email, live chat, or social media.

2. Doing your best to address client complaints and issues, if necessary, elevate them to a manager or supervisor.

3. Use customer relationship management (CRM) software to track and record customer interactions and questions.

4. Assisting consumers with order placement or technical problem-solving.

5. Providing details on goods or services, such as cost and accessibility.

6. Retaining a high degree of expertise in products and services to serve customers.

7. Contributing to the enhancement of procedures and guidelines for customer service.

An online customer service representative's overall objective is to give exceptional customer service and support to assist in problem-solving and enhance the client experience.

Skills needed for customer service

These vital customer service skills are listed below:

1. Clear communication skills are a must for customer service agents, whether they communicate with clients face-to-face, over the phone, or by email.

2. Problem-solving abilities: A large part of customer service is dealing with client complaints and having the flexibility to think quickly and come up with solutions.

3. Empathy: A key component of providing good customer service is to relate to the emotions and worries of a client.

4. Patience: Dealing with customers can be difficult, so it's crucial to have the patience to listen to their issues and assist them.

5. Flexibility: It's critical to be flexible and adaptable because customer support employees may need to manage a variety of questions and problems.

6. Organizational abilities: It's crucial to be well-organized and successfully manage your time because customer service professionals frequently need to keep track of several projects and conversations.

7. Computer skills: Since many customer service positions include software and computer systems, it's critical to have a solid understanding of technology.

Technical expertise and interpersonal skills are needed to provide outstanding customer service.

It's crucial to speak with consumers clearly and sympathetically and use your organizational and problem-solving abilities to fix problems and enhance the customer experience.

How to get started in customer service

Here are some measures you can take if you want to start a career in customer service:

1. Gain experience: Working part-time or seasonal employment in retail, food service, or other client-facing professions will help you get crucial expertise in customer service.

2. Take education and training into account. While many customer service positions call for a high school diploma or equivalent, some may include further education or training. Enroll in classes in business, communications, or customer service.

3. Create your resume: Emphasize any customer service experience, pertinent education, or abilities in your resume. You might also wish to list credentials, like one in customer service.

4. Start applying for jobs: Start submitting applications for customer service positions that match your qualifications. To get your foot in the door and develop experience in the industry, apply for entry-level roles.

Launching a career in customer service calls for a combination of education, experience, and tenacity. You may improve your chances of getting the perfect customer service job by developing your resume, networking, and acquiring relevant skills.

How to find online customer service jobs

You can locate online customer service jobs in the following ways:

1. Job websites: Sites like Indeed, Monster, and LinkedIn are just a few that feature customer service positions. You may frequently look for employment on these websites based on geography, job title, and other factors.

2. Company websites: It can be worthwhile to visit the careers or jobs section of various platforms to see if they

have any customer service positions since many businesses publish their job openings there.

3. Professional associations: A few associations, including the International Association of Customer Service Professionals, maintain job boards with listings for employment in the customer service industry.

4. Networking: In the customer service sector, networking can be a method to discover employment openings and establish relationships. Think about contacting professionals you know or going to job fairs and other professional gatherings.

5. Cold calling: If a company doesn't have any customer service job vacancies advertised and you are interested in working there, you can try calling them to find out if there are any open positions. Adapting your cover letter and resume to the organization and job you're interested in can be helpful.

In general, it's vital to adopt techniques to locate online customer service employment. You may improve your chances of obtaining the ideal employment by using job websites, networking, and other resources.

CHAPTER 8

Online Writing and Editing Jobs for Teens

Online writing is the process of producing written material on a computer or other internet-connected device. Writing for websites, blogs, social media, email, and other online channels can fall under this category. Additionally, it could entail writing the text for electronic documents like Google Docs or PDFs.

Online editing involves revising written material produced for an online platform. It entails editing the content's structure and organization to make it effective and proofreading it for spelling and grammar errors.

Online editing can be done by the author or by a different editor. It entails using various tools, including word processing programs, content management systems, or online editing platforms.

Types of online writing and editing jobs for teens

Teens may be qualified for various online writing and editing jobs depending on their interests, qualifications, and experience. Here are a few instances:

1. Blogging: Many teenagers find blogging a fun and engaging avenue to express their ideas, stories, and hobbies. They can start their blog using a blogging platform like Blogger or WordPress. They can also write as a guest author for an already-existing site.

2. Social media management: Companies and organizations use teenagers to run their social media pages, which includes writing and scheduling posts, interacting with followers, and keeping track of analytics.

3. Freelance writing: Teens with excellent writing abilities can work as independent writers, producing content for websites, periodicals, and other media.

4. Editing and proofreading: Teens with an attention to detail and solid grammatical abilities can offer their services as editors or proofreaders, evaluating and revising written work to ensure its accuracy, clarity, and usage of language.

5. Content production: Companies and groups use teenagers to produce written or graphic content for their websites or social media accounts. It entails infographics, blog entries, product descriptions, or other material.

Tips for finding and succeeding in online writing and editing work

Listed below are some pointers for locating and excelling at online writing and editing jobs:

1. Improve your abilities: Effective online writing and editing require good writing and editing abilities. It entails enrolling in writing or editing classes, reading writing manuals and advice, and routinely writing and editing to hone your abilities.

2. Create a portfolio. Show prospective clients or employers a portfolio of your writing and editing work by compiling it. Be sure to save your best work as you complete writing and editing assignments so that you can add it to your portfolio.

3. Network and establish connections: Contacts can be crucial in locating online writing and editing jobs. To expand your network, join writing or editing organizations, go to trade shows, and get in touch with other authors and editors.

4. Use job boards and freelance websites. Websites like Upwork, Freelancer, and ProBlogger are just a few examples of those that provide online writing and editing employment.

5. Be professional: It's critical to project professionalism and dependability when writing and editing online. It includes sticking to deadlines, communicating, and producing excellent work.

CHAPTER 9

Online Design and Creativity Jobs for Teens

Online design and creativity jobs entail using artistic talent and design methodologies to produce visual content for various uses, including websites, advertisements, social media posts, and marketing materials.

These tasks can be completed remotely, either as freelancers or as a member of a company's remote staff. In online design and creativity, job titles include graphic designer, web designer, social media manager, and content creator.

Digital assets, pictures, graphics, and videos require design software like Adobe Creative Suite or Canva.

Examples of online design and creativity jobs for teens

Listed below are a few teen-friendly examples of internet design and creative jobs:

1. Graphic designer: This position entails producing hand-drawn or computer-generated graphic concepts to convey ideas that enthrall, educate, or inspire clients. A graphic designer can provide marketing materials, website graphics, logos, and more.

2. Social Media Manager: In this position, you'll create and oversee a business's social media presence, post updates and engage with followers. Social media managers may design social media marketing initiatives and assess their efficacy.

3. Material Creator: In this position, you would create and curate written, visual, or video content for a business's website or social media pages. It entails producing blog entries, infographics, memes, or other visual content.

4. Web designer: This position entails creating websites for people or companies. Web designers create a website's layout, color scheme, and appearance.

5. Online tutor: If you are skilled in a subject, consider working as an online tutor. In this position, virtual sessions assist students in learning and comprehending a subject.

Teaching credentials or expertise in design software, for example, may be necessary for some of these professions, so keep that in mind. Create a portfolio of your work to show prospective employers what you have accomplished.

Tips for finding and succeeding in online design and creativity work

Listed below are some pointers for locating and excelling in online design and creativity work:

1. Compile your work into a portfolio. For design and employment, you must have an online portfolio of your previous work. Your portfolio should feature your best work and showcase your abilities.

2. Keep up with industry trends: For professional and relevant work, it's critical to be informed about the most recent developments in design and innovation. It entails participating in online classes or workshops, reading trade publications, and keeping up with social media activity.

3. Network and establish connections: Networking can be particularly crucial for locating these positions.

Consider interacting with other professionals on LinkedIn or other social media sites, at conferences and events, and joining groups or organizations for your field.

4. Develop your marketing skills. As a small business owner or freelancer, it's crucial to know how to advertise your services and yourself. It entails developing a website or social media presence, producing marketing collateral, and connecting with prospective customers.

5. Be adaptable and receptive to criticism: Working with clients and stakeholders to produce the best potential outcome is part of online design and innovation work. Be receptive to criticism and prepared to make adjustments or edits as necessary.

6. Maintain organization and time management skills: Working alone might be difficult, maintain organization and time management skills. Deliver tasks by adopting project management software like Trello or Asana.

CHAPTER 10

Virtual assisting Jobs for Teens

Virtual assistance positions involve helping clients remotely, usually online. Numerous duties fall under the purview of virtual assistants, such as monitoring social media accounts, performing research, setting up appointments, and responding to emails.

Jobs for virtual assistants can work as freelancers or contract basis, and they can work for different clients or a single employer. People that are organized, detail-oriented, and able to operate independently are a good fit for virtual assistant employment.

They might be a suitable fit for persons who want the freedom of working from home or are seeking a job that allows for remote work.

Types of virtual assistance jobs available to teens

Teenagers may be able to find a variety of virtual assistant employment. Options to consider include:

1. Social media management: It involves postings for social media accounts, planning them out, interacting with followers, and monitoring analytics.

2. Customer service: Virtual assistants involve responding to inquiries from clients, resolving problems, or guiding them to the right resources.

3. Data entry involves entering information into a database or spreadsheet from paper documents or electronic files.

4. Researcher: Virtual assistants involve online research to compile data on various subjects.

5. Planning events: Virtual assistants may be in charge of arranging and scheduling events, reserving locations and vendors, setting up budgets, and distributing invitations.

6. Transcribing audio or video recordings into written documentation, also known as transcription.

7. Personal assistant: Virtual assistants could be required to manage a calendar, make travel arrangements, or schedule appointments.

It's vital to understand that some prerequisites or restrictions, such as being at least 18 years old or possessing education or experience, may apply to certain virtual assistant positions.

How to become a virtual assistant

1. Identify your interests and skills: Identity the tasks that fit your skill and relevant training or schooling you may have. It will aid you in deciding which areas of virtual assistance are for your qualification.

2. Make a portfolio of your work. To demonstrate your abilities and expertise, gather examples of your work, such as writing samples, design projects, or customer service encounters.

3. Create a website: A website can help you build your brand and make it simpler for potential customers to discover more about your services.

4. Think about being certified: There are several qualifications available for virtual assistants, such as the Certified Virtual Assistant (CVA) or the Virtual Administrative Consultant (VAC).

Certification may increase your marketability to potential clients and show your dedication to the industry.

5. Find clients: There are numerous ways to do so as a virtual assistant, including through freelance job boards, social media, or networking. You can also reach out to entrepreneurs or small business owners who might require online support.

6. Set your rates: Choose the amount you want to bill clients for your services based on your expertise, experience, and the going rate for services of a similar nature in your neighborhood.

Don't forget to account for all your charges, such as any operating expenses for your business.

Platforms and companies that hire virtual assistants

1. Upwork: Upwork is a platform that links freelancers with clients who need their services. It consists of numerous categories, such as virtual help, and enables independent contractors to choose their hours and pay rates.

2. Fiverr: Fiverr is a website where independent contractors can list various services, including virtual support. Users can peruse many offerings and select the one that best suits their needs.

3. Zirtual: Zirtual is a company that uses virtual assistants to help customers with various tasks, including scheduling, email management, and social media management.

4. Time Etc.: This business offers virtual assistants to clients across the globe. It provides many services, such as data input, customer support, and social media management.

5. Virtual Staff Finder: This service assists companies in locating and hiring virtual assistants. It provides various services, such as data input, customer support, and social media management.

6. Belay Solutions: Belay Solutions is a business that offers virtual assistants to assist with duties that include managing calendars, emails, and data input.

These are just a few platforms and businesses that employ virtual assistants; there are many more. Investigate your options to locate the one that best meets your needs.

Tips for success as a virtual assistant

As a virtual assistant, you can succeed by following these pointers:

1. Concentrate on your strong points. Make an effort to focus on the activities that describe your skill.

2. Develop a professional network: As a virtual assistant, networking can be essential for locating new clients and job prospects. Network and meet people, participate in professional groups, or go to industry-related events.

3. Be trustworthy and quick to respond: As a virtual assistant, have trustworthiness and response times for your clients. To do this, you must adhere to deadlines, communicate clearly, and be accessible to your clients.

4. Maintain organization: Providing virtual support may require juggling several clients and duties. To meet client expectations, maintain organization, and keep track of your deadlines.

5. Be willing to learn: Because virtual aid is changing, it's critical to pick new knowledge and tools. To keep current and enhance your services, take online courses or go to industry events.

6. Establish clear boundaries with your clients. Setting boundaries with your clients can help maintain a work-life balance. It entails creating weekly work-hour restrictions or laying down specific guidelines for communication and availability.

These pointers can help you position yourself to succeed as a virtual assistant.

CHAPTER 11

Tips for finding and applying for online jobs

You can find authentic internet employment possibilities by following a few basic procedures, which are as follows:

1. Conduct online research on the business to confirm its legitimacy. Check the company's website and social media profiles, look for feedback from current or past employees, and verify if the business is legit.

2. Search for caution signs: If a job offer asks you for sensitive personal information like your social security number or bank account details, or if you have to pay a fee to apply, be skeptical.

3. Use trustworthy job search portals: Many websites list online employment prospects, but not all are trustworthy. Consider LinkedIn, Indeed, and Glassdoor as some excellent choices.

4. Establish a network with individuals in your industry: Contact people you know and ask if they are aware of any online employment chances. The people in your network may know about job openings.

5. Think about working with a staffing agency: Staffing companies can be a fantastic way to obtain temporary or contract work and can assist you in finding opportunities that correspond with your abilities and expertise.

How to create a professional online presence

If you want to establish a credible web presence, follow these steps:

1. Use a professional email address: People generally see your email address first when they receive correspondence from you, so it's crucial to use a professional-sounding email address. Avoid utilizing addresses with too many nicknames, digits, or addresses that are too casual.

2. Build your LinkedIn profile. LinkedIn is a platform for professional networking that gives you access to contacts in your industry.

Create a LinkedIn profile and start building your network to find professional opportunities and establish yourself as a thought leader.

3. Have a personal website: If you have the ability or area of interest, set up a website to promote your accomplishments and display your work.

How to construct a powerful online application

Here are some pointers for crafting online job applications:

1. Comply with the directions for the application Application guidelines must be read and followed. Be sure to follow any instructions the employer gives you regarding the structure or content of your resume.

2. Adapt your application to the position: Use specific examples to show how you fit the qualifications mentioned in the job description and emphasize your abilities and expertise that are most applicable to the role.

3. Use a professional format: Make sure your cover letter and resume have a professional appearance and are free of spelling and punctuation errors.

4. Be succinct: Keep your cover letter and resume to a manageable length and leave out any extraneous details. Use bullet points to make it simple to scan.

5. Follow-up: It's acceptable to send a cordial follow-up email to the company to find out the status of your application if you haven't heard back from them after a few weeks. It demonstrates your interest in the job and can help the company remember your application.

Success strategies for online employment

As technology advances and more people look for flexible employment opportunities, online jobs are becoming more and more popular. While there are advantages to working online, there can also be drawbacks.

These suggestions will help you succeed in your virtual employment, from time management to communication abilities and goal planning.

1. Time management: One of the most valuable aspects of working online is keeping a good work-life balance. Even while working 24/7 can be enticing, it's crucial to establish limits and follow a schedule. To help you keep organized and on task, adopt a time management tool, such as a calendar or app.

2. Communication abilities: In any work, communication is essential, but in an online setting where you might not always have the chance to engage with people in person, communication becomes more necessary.

Communicate your thoughts and ideas, and respond promptly to emails and messages from your coworkers and clients.

3. Establishing objectives and monitoring progress: Setting clear objectives is crucial for success in any employment, including online work. Setting goals can keep you motivated and engaged. To stay on track, think about adopting a goal-tracking tool or app.

4. Use technology: Various tools and technologies can improve productivity and efficiency while working from home.

Use these technologies to help you keep organized and connected with your team, such as project management software, collaboration tools, and online meeting platforms.

5. Take breaks: When working online, it's simple to become overwhelmed by your workload, but it's vital to relax and re-energize. Go for a little stroll, stretch, or do something calming once you step away from your computer. You'll be more productive in the long term if you take breaks.

6. Designate a workspace: Designate a location in your house dedicated to working and is not shared with your living or recreation spaces. You'll be able to establish a professional environment and psychologically get ready for work with this.

Ascertain that your workspace has all you require to perform your job successfully, including adequate lighting and comfort.

7. Maintain a connection with your team: Working alone can occasionally feel isolated, so it's critical to maintain a link with your team.

Try to maintain communication with your coworkers, whether it be through routine check-ins or online team-building exercises. You'll experience a sense of community and support.

8. Establish boundaries with friends and family: Establish limits with your friends and family and let them know your availability and working hours. It enables you to concentrate on your work and cut off outside distractions.

9. Keep up with changes in your field: It's critical to keep up with new trends and advancements in your sector.

10. Remain motivated: Working online can make it simple to lose drive, especially if you don't have the same structure and resources at your disposal as you would in a conventional office. Set short, doable, and gratifying goals to stay motivated.

CHAPTER 12

How to get paid as a freelancer

There are numerous ways to get paid as a freelancer for your work. Typical choices include:

1. Bank transfer: This is a typical way freelancers get paid. The person or business paying you will send the money immediately into your account after receiving your bank account details from you.

2. Online payment platforms: PayPal, Payoneer, Stripe, and Square are just a few of the many online payment platforms that let you get paid for your services. These platforms accept payments from many parts of the world.

3. Digital wallets: With a digital wallet, you may store several payment methods in one location and accept payments via your phone or other devices. Examples of such wallets include Apple Pay and Google Pay.

There are numerous systems for receiving payment; these are but a few examples. Investigate your options to locate the best one that suits your requirements and objectives.

CHAPTER 13

Success stories of teens who have found success in online jobs

Teens may make extra money and obtain work experience through online jobs. In this part, we'll spotlight a few successful teenagers who've had success with internet jobs.

1. Zach Luye: At age 13, Zach launched his own company making unique graphics and drawings for customers online. Since then, he has expanded his company with a group of designers.

2. Emma Moyes: At age 16, Emma opened her own Etsy store selling accessories and jewelry handcrafted by herself. She has sold over 10,000 units.

3. Alina Morse: At age 9, Alina launched her own company, producing a line of nutritious candies known as "Zollipops." Since then, her business has expanded, and her products are now available in shops.

4. Nick D'Aloisio - At age 15, Nick created the "Summly" app. When he was barely 17, he sold the software to Yahoo for millions of dollars.

5. Jake Olson - At age 16, Jake launched his own company. He designs graphics and websites for customers. Since then, he has expanded his company.

6. Jack Obrochta: A 19-year-old with a thriving online tutoring business that he launched while still a high school student. His online tutoring platform assists other students with their exam study and academic progress.

7. Rosie Reid: Rosie Reid, a 19-year-old entrepreneur, sells handmade invitations and greeting cards on Etsy. She has a profitable internet business highlighted in publications and television.

CHAPTER 14

Conclusion

In conclusion, obtaining an online job as a teen can be a fantastic way to earn money from home and gain work experience. Teens can work online in many fields, such as social media management, freelance writing, and online tutoring.

Finding an online job that matches your abilities and interests should take some time, as you will be more likely to succeed and enjoy your work if you do.

You can discover and excel in an online job using various resources, including job boards and professional development programs. You may use these resources to your advantage while you navigate the job market and advance your career by giving you information and help.

You should be concerned about your online safety and privacy when searching for online jobs as a possible source of income. Use secure passwords to prevent potential fraud or scams.

In general, doing work online may be a flexible and satisfying method for teenagers to make money and get skills. You may position yourself for success in your online career by taking the time to discover an online job that matches your interests.